THE CONSULTING WAY

THE CONSULTING WAY

A Guide to Becoming a Successful Management Consultant

ERIK GAUSEL

ILLUSTRATIONS: MAGNUS HERMSTAD

iUniverse LLC
Bloomington

The Consulting Way
A Guide to Becoming a Successful
Management Consultant

iUniverse books may be ordered through booksellers or by contacting:

iUniverse LLC
1663 Liberty Drive
Bloomington, IN 47403
www.iuniverse.com
1-800-Authors (1-800-288-4677)

Because of the dynamic nature of the Internet, any web addresses or links contained in this book may have changed since publication and may no longer be valid. The views expressed in this work are solely those of the author and do not necessarily reflect the views of the publisher, and the publisher hereby disclaims any responsibility for them.

Any people depicted in stock imagery provided by Thinkstock are models, and such images are being used for illustrative purposes only. Certain stock imagery © Thinkstock

ISBN: 978-1-4759-9810-8 (sc)
ISBN: 978-1-4759-9809-2 (ebk)

Library of Congress Control Number: 2013912543

Printed in the United States of America

iUniverse rev. date: 08/02/2013

Contents

Preface

Help! I'm a management consultant! That's how I felt in April 1986 when I started working in Arthur Andersen's Management Information Consulting Division, later Andersen Consulting (and now Accenture).

What did I know about management consulting? Absolutely nothing! Why did I go to work at Andersen? Pure coincidence! They were the first company to offer me a job during my final year of business school, and it sounded like a great place to start my career.

Luckily for me, the Arthur Andersen system invested heavily in training new recruits. Step by step, through a variety of engagements in many industries (financial services, transport, and the public sector), I learned what it took to become a management consultant. Every year there was compulsory training in St. Charles, Illinois, at the Arthur Andersen training centre, where I attended courses adapted to career development in management consulting.

Today, twenty-seven years later, I'm still consulting. Most likely, I will be a management consultant until I retire. It is a challenging and rewarding career, and for me it has become a way of life.

Over the years, I've thought many times about writing a book about management consulting. When researching the topic, I found that there are numerous articles and textbooks of an academic nature. And if you want to learn how to start and grow your own consulting business, you have several books to choose from.

However, when it boils down to what management consultants actually do and how they work, most of the literature is kept in-house, behind closed doors, in the libraries of the great global management consultancy firms.

So if you don't happen to work in one of these companies, there's not much available. This is what inspired me to write *The Consulting Way.* It's an attempt to communicate the essence of management consulting in a practical and, hopefully, easy-to-understand way. This book is for anyone who wants to understand and learn the basics of the very powerful consulting approach.

The pocket-sized format allows you to take the book everywhere and use it on a daily basis when working the consulting way.

Introduction

What Is a Management Consultant?

The word "consulting" comes from Latin (*consultare*, "to discuss"). Throughout history, leaders have been surrounded by expert advisors to discuss important issues, enabling them to make informed decisions.

These days, it seems that everyone's a consultant. The broad definition basically covers anyone who gets paid for giving advice. Millions of people have the title "consultant" in some form on their business card. There are probably several hundred thousand management consultants.

But what separates the management consultant from the consulting herd? There is no precise definition. But I share the view that a management consultant (at least a good one) gives *strategic* advice to *top* and *high-level management*. Here we have set some boundaries for what kind of advice (strategic) is given and to which target audience (top and high-level management).

What Will You Gain from Reading This Book?

Whether you are a management consultant, a consultant wannabe, or a line manager, you will be more successful by learning and practicing the consulting way of working.

Are you considering a career in management consulting? Chapter 1 provides an overview of what management consultants do. Chapter 2 focuses on how to become a good management consultant.

For the practitioner, chapters 3 and 4 dig into the two key areas of expertise that are expected from every management consultant: problem solving and project management. The fresh consultant should get a good feel for these basic topics, while the more experienced can refresh their knowledge and use the content as a checklist or mini-encyclopaedia.

Chapter 5 focuses on how to secure continuous learning and development as a management consultant. This is extremely important for those who are looking for a long-term consulting career.

Chapter 6 highlights important changes in the management consulting industry. What put bread and butter on the consultant's table in the past won't necessarily be enough in the future. The successful management consultant must understand these industry changes and adapt to them.

This is not a complete textbook on how to become a great management consultant. Nor is it a complete guide to all the tools and techniques that great consultants have in their toolkit. For those eager to learn more, I have provided a list of recommended reading materials at the end of this book.

CHAPTER 1

What Does a Management Consultant Do?

1.1 Why Do Companies Hire Consultants?

Never, Always, or Sometimes?

"Why would anyone in his or her right mind hire a management consultant?" This is a point of view that many executives have, especially executives who are used to succeeding. They may see hiring a consultant as a symptom of failure. They may feel that there is a problem that they're not able to solve or that their leadership abilities are weak.

On the opposite end of the scale, there are executives who are overly dependent on consultants. No major decisions can be made without seeking advice from an external consultant, and all strategic projects are led by consulting teams.

There is no optimal model for how much consulting a company requires. It depends on the company's situation and management's knowledge and experience. Most companies will, however, benefit from using consulting services from time to time.

When to Consider Hiring a Consultant

Someone once said, "Insanity is doing the same thing over and over again and expecting different results." Customer satisfaction may be declining, sales dropping, or costs escalating. If management has prior experience with successfully addressing a major business problem, they may be well equipped to solve a similar one.

If, however, a completely new situation arises, previous experiences may not be sufficient. Maybe the company is in a mature industry, and new competitors have started targeting the most profitable customer segments with new product offerings or distribution channels.

Perhaps the industry is undergoing major restructuring, and there is a need to consider merger and acquisition options. Or maybe the business is experiencing difficulties of a more operational nature that they haven't been able to resolve.

The consulting market is huge and continually expanding. There are many providers of management consultancy services. No matter which industry, function, or phase a company is in, there are management consultants ready to help.

There will always be a market for consultants. In prosperous times, consultants are called upon to develop growth strategies. During recessions, consultants enter the arena to assist in consolidation and cost cutting. Consultants may also be asked to give advice on how to continue to be successful.

Case: For several years, the market leader in the retail banking sector had been losing market share in mortgage loans, especially among first-time homeowners. A new and attractively priced loan product had been launched and was being marketed expertly.

Salespeople were trained in how to sell the new loan, and good incentive systems were in place. A web solution had been in place for several years to effectively handle online loan applications. New loan customers were very satisfied with the product, but market share continued to decline.

Finally, an external consultant was hired to analyse the whole loan process to find the cause of the problem. The analysis showed several problems that management was unaware of: (1) The bank's call centre could not handle the large number of phone calls from loan applicants. Customers were put on hold, and many prospective customers hung up. (2) To save costs, the call centre referred loan applicants to the online loan application form. Testing proved that the form was technically unstable and very complex to fill in. These problems resulted in many prospects giving up during the application process.

After being presented with the fact-based analysis from the consultant, showing how many prospective customers were lost due to deficiencies in the call centre and web solution, a comprehensive action plan was implemented, and sales slowly started to rise.

1.2 What Does the Consultant Have to Offer?

What Does the Consultant Bring to the Table?

In general, management consultants are experts in identifying, diagnosing, and solving business problems. They are trained to pinpoint a problem and suggest solutions for fixing it.

The consultant is an external and objective third party who can bring in an outside view, unbiased with regards to internal politics in the organization and emotions of management. When consultants have the relevant experience, know-how, and wisdom, they can often find ways of doing things differently.

What Are the Consultant's Goals?

Obviously, management consultants want to get paid and collect their fee. To achieve this, at least over time, the consultant has to deliver value for money to the customer. The perceived values must be greater than the consulting fees incurred. This usually means that the business will become more successful after implementing the consultant's advice than it was prior to hiring the consultant.

The goal of the consultant should, however, always be the same: help the customer become more successful. A successful customer will be satisfied and more than happy to pay the consultant's fee.

"The new strategy will increase
market share and profits!"

1.3 Why Is Change Important?

Why Change?

Since the beginning of time, change has been going on; it is a never-ending process. In business, change is happening everywhere: increasing globalization, new technology, new industries, and new business models. Change can seldom be stopped, but many do their best to slow things down.

There must be balance between the amount of change inside the organization and the business environment. When the rate of change inside the business becomes slower than outside, the end is near. The only question is when. So, to be successful over time, every organization has to continually adapt to its business environment.

What Is Change?

Change can be viewed in many perspectives. A simplified way of viewing change is the scope of it:

1. Small (incremental) changes continually improve the business and align it to requirements from the environment. This requires good managers who, together with their employees, always look for more effective and efficient solutions.
2. Large changes require entirely new solutions and ways of working. This means a lot of hard

work to analyse and evaluate alternatives before deciding on the right solution to implement. Project groups and change management skills are usually needed.

Change Agents

All consultants are dependent on change. Change is fuel for the consulting engine. One could argue that without change, there would be no need for consultants to give advice or participate in projects.

Consultants can be viewed as change agents, hired to assist organizations in their change process in one way or another. The consultant's purpose is to help the customer change to become more successful.

"A massive change is underway. All agents respond!"

1.4 What Services Do Consultants Provide?

Many see consultants as potatoes—they can be utilized in many different ways and cover different needs. Professional customers will have a very precise description of what kind of consultant they are looking for and what service the consultant will provide.

The Expert

Sometimes, consultants will be called upon to give their expert advice or opinion. The consultant may have in-depth knowledge about a certain function (M&A, finance, etc.) or a specific situation or process. Typical questions for the consultant include, "What is the best solution to the issue at hand?" and "How do you suggest that we proceed?"

The Process Driver

Very often, the organization will possess the necessary skills and knowledge to solve a problem. But they may require an experienced and independent consultant to lead the process of finding a good solution.

To be a good process driver, having experience from similar situations is an advantage, as is having sufficient time to ensure that planning, involvement of key personnel, necessary analysis, workshops, and documentation are performed, thereby ensuring a good process.

"I recommend selling the international retail business to focus on core business at home."

"You want involvement? Then all departments have to be represented at the brainstorming session."

Management for Hire

For important projects or programs, management will want an experienced project or program manager to lead the work. Very often, a standalone consultant or a consulting team will be hired to secure successful project management. But consultants are also sometimes hired to fill ordinary line manager positions for a defined period of time, for example, if the manager moves to a new position, and there is no good candidate in the department to fill the gap while hiring a new candidate. Hiring consultants as management for hire is often used to test out a candidate the organization is considering hiring on a permanent basis.

Quality Assurance (QA)

In high-risk situations (for example, introducing a mission-critical IT system), management should consider using a consultant for independent walkthroughs of the solution, process, or project. This will secure an unbiased opinion and aid in uncovering risks. In large IT projects, you will often find one consultant (or consulting team) leading the project, while another consultant functions as the quality assurer. The quality assurer will usually interview people in and around the project and do structured reviews of project documentation. Findings will be documented in a QA report and presented to management.

"Pete's leaving the firm? Don't panic. I can step in for three months and head the accounting department."

"To meet the project deadline, the team needs two additional programmers. By the way, the coffee machine's broken."

The Facilitator

Quite often, a consultant will be called upon to function as an independent or neutral facilitator of discussions or workshops. The facilitator will lead the meeting or workshop and ensure a good process. This is similar to being a process driver but downsized to functioning in a meeting or workshop. The facilitator will often be asked to secure necessary documentation and will therefore often bring in a colleague as documentation support (secretary).

The Secretary

All projects require documentation. The final results (recommendations, implementation plans, etc.) must be comprehensively documented. This is necessary to ensure that decisions are based on facts and well-founded arguments. Documentation also works as handover material to the people who are going to implement the consultant's recommendations.

In addition, a project will require temporary documentation to drive the project forward. Mandates and plans, minutes from meetings, action logs, and so on are necessary to ensure effective communication and efficient follow-up. The secretary (or "documentor") is therefore an important role in all projects, meetings, and workshops.

It's challenging to be a good secretary. To make sure everyone's on the same page, take time to summarize decisions and open issues before pushing forward.

"We'll look into challenges later, Alice. Now let's explore the possibilities in Bob's suggestion."

"We need more resources." "No time for that, we just need to work longer hours." "We need more coffee!"

CHAPTER 2

How to Become a Management Consultant

2.1 Starting Out on a Consulting Career

How to Start Out on a Consulting Career

The traditional way of becoming a management consultant is to join one of the large and well-known consulting firms after finishing your university degree. Companies like Accenture, McKinsey, and the Boston Consulting Group provide formal training, methodologies, and customer engagements where you can learn the consulting trade one step at a time. There are great career opportunities in these pyramid-oriented firms.

Typical Consulting career structure (pyramid)

You may start as an analyst, but when you develop and prove your skills, you will be promoted to consultant, senior consultant, and manager or principal. The most successful may even be offered a partnership. The structured approaches and work ethics you learn are beneficial no matter what you choose to do later in your career.

Consulting can also be a career choice for very highly experienced managers. There are many niche consulting firms that provide specialized advisory services or management-for-hire to their clients. They expect their hires to be masters within their fields. These firms may have their own methodologies, but their competitive strength is usually the very high expertise level of their consultants. They therefore spend little resources training their employees but expect them to draw on their own experiences from successful careers in management.

Consulting Is Harder Than It Looks

With experience and training, many become good consultants. However, like in all other occupations, only a few become truly great.

Not everyone succeeds as a consultant. It's never about not being smart enough. It usually boils down to a lack of understanding the consulting role, which will be described in section 2.2. You have to know what to do and when to do it. You also have to learn what to say and when to say it. Timing is very important.

A lack of understanding of the consulting role can be magnified by insufficient interpersonal skills (section 2.3) or not being able (or willing) to learn the necessary technical skills (section 2.4).

2.2 The Consulting Role

Being a consultant requires a thorough understanding of your role. As a consultant, you are first and foremost an advisor. A consultant gives advice, but it is the client who makes decisions based on the consultant's recommendations.

The following is expected from you in the role of consultant:

o **Integrity and accountability.** You mean what you say and believe in your recommendations. Someone once said, "Integrity is the holy grail of consulting." And Arthur Andersen said, "Think straight, talk straight."
o **Objectivity.** You collect facts, perform analysis, and make unbiased recommendations.
o **Professionalism.** The content and packaging of your work into deliverables is of high quality.
o **Credibility.** Recommendations you present are plausible and believable. Facts and fact-based analysis give you the necessary credibility. You focus on meeting or exceeding the customer's expectations.
o **Confidentiality.** You handle all information and results with great care and do not reveal them to others without prior consent from the customer.
o **Value for money.** Your contributions and results substantially exceed the fees the customer pays.

"Being a consultant is much harder than I thought."

2.3 Interpersonal Skills

A consultant gives advice when asked for it. You are not expected to run around telling everyone what you think they should do. As previously discussed, you have to understand not only what to say and do but when.

To succeed as a consultant, you therefore have to develop excellent interpersonal skills:

o **Active listening.** You ask questions and use the answers to gather valuable information about the issue at hand, the organization, its practices, and its people.
o **Flexibility.** You are easy to get along with and look for solutions instead of problems.
o **Availability.** You are easy to get hold of and respond quickly to phone messages and e-mail requests.
o **Timeliness.** You show up ten minutes before meetings and prepare so that the meeting can start on time.
o **Agility.** You adapt to working in different types of teams, often put together from several organizational units.
o **Communicative.** You present your recommendations in a structured and trustworthy manner. You always have your elevator pitch ready so that you can explain to anyone, in a few words, what the essence of a problem or solution is.

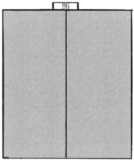

"We're considering outsourcing, but also
offshoring the back office to our office in Poland.
The final recommendation will be presented
to the management team in three weeks."

2.4 Technical Skills

In addition to a good understanding of the consulting role and having good interpersonal skills, the management consultant also needs to master technical skills:

- o **Problem solving.** You are analytical and have a structured approach for defining a problem, structuring it, and solving it.
- o **Project management.** Since almost all consulting engagements become projects, you are skilled in participating in and leading projects.
- o **Documentation tools.** As a consultant, you will usually be responsible for writing minutes, crunching numbers, and building presentation material, so it is important to be proficient in text editors (such as Word), spreadsheets (Excel), and presentation tools (PowerPoint).
- o **Methodology.** You will often be chosen as a consultant based on having a structured approach or method (for example, a business strategy methodology) for the business issue to be solved.
- o **Knowledge about the business issue.** Even though you are not an industry or functional expert, the customer expects you to have a good grasp of the business issue you are

working on. This is why most consultants over time develop expertise in a limited number of areas. "Content is king" means there has to be real substance in the recommendations that are made to management.

2.5 The X Factor of Great Consultants

What is the X factor that differentiates the great consultants from the rest of the pack? Is there a consulting gene that some people are born with? Can it be learned? I don't have a definitive answer to these questions, but I do believe that to have consulting as a long-term career that makes you happy and your customers satisfied, you need the following qualities or skills:

o **The client comes first.** You put the interests of your customers before your own personal interests. Keep your ego in your pocket. You are getting paid to help the customer be successful, not to be right.

o **Genuine interest in helping others.** You get pleasure from seeing your customers and consulting colleagues succeed without having to get formal recognition for your own contribution (although this is always welcome).

o **Ability to engage others.** Your knowledge and enthusiasm creates energy when interacting with the customer.

o **Creative and imaginative.** You find new solutions or ways of searching for them, making you a sought-after advisor and facilitator.

o **Trust builder.** You are able to build deep trust with customers and colleagues.

o **Curious and continuously learning.** You are always eager to explore new ideas and approaches.

"You can accomplish anything in life, provided that you do not mind who gets the credit."

– Harry S. Truman (1884–1972, USA's 33rd president)

"When a great consultant is present, problems are solved. And the customer learns how to solve problems on his/her own in the future."

(unknown)

"My grandfather once told me that there are two kinds of people: those who work and those who take the credit. He told me to try to be in the first group; there was less competition there."

– Indira Gandhi (1917–1984), prime minister of India

"A customer is the most important visitor on our premises. He is not dependent on us; we are dependent on him. He is not an interruption on our work; he is the purpose of it. He is not an outsider on our business; he is a part of it. We are not doing him a favor by serving him; He is giving us an opportunity to do so."

– Mahatma Gandhi (1869–1948), Indian leader

2.6 How Do Consultants Work?

We have already established that there are many types of management consultants. They have different areas of expertise and work with customers at all levels of management.

But there is common ground. There are fundamentals that all management consultants will agree to:

1. *Problem solving:* The ability to solve business problems individually and in a team environment.
2. *Project management:* Almost all consulting engagements are project based, and as a consultant, you are expected to be a project expert.

The following chapters give an introduction to problem solving (chapter 3) and project management (chapter 4). They will not immediately make you an expert in these disciplines, but they will give you a fundamental grasp of the two topics.

Courses and on-the-job training are required to become an expert project manager or problem-solving artist.

CHAPTER 3

How to Solve Problems

3.1 Introduction to Problem Solving

There Is Always a Problem

No matter what a customer says, there is always a problem. It could be a fundamental strategic problem or a minor operational problem. But rest assured, a problem there is! If not, you wouldn't be there in the first place.

What Is Problem Solving?

As a consultant, you are expected to be an excellent problem solver. You may be thinking, *That sounds good. I'm a smart person. We solved tons of cases at business school. How hard can it be?*

You may be right. Maybe you have what it takes to solve a customer's business problems. A good problem solver has

- analytical skills,
- a toolkit,
- a structured approach or process, and
- people skills.

You may be nodding as you read the first three bullets. But a puzzled look may have appeared on your face when you read "people skills." What do people skills have to do with problem solving? We'll get into that shortly (section 3.7). First, let's dig into the hard-core analytical stuff.

3.2 The Problem-Solving Process

Problem solving is a structured and solution-oriented process. There are four main steps in the problem-solving process:

1. **Defining the problem:** Finding the key question to be answered and the scope of the process.
2. **Structuring the problem:** Breaking the problem down into logical components that can be analysed.
3. **Analysis:** Developing the storyline and solution hypothesis and performing the necessary analysis.
4. **Verification and presentation:** Verifying the results with key stakeholders, developing the report, and presenting the recommendations to the customer.

We'll dive into each step using an example that many can relate to.

Linda, the head of a client's facilities management department, has come to you with a problem. She is getting swamped with e-mails from frustrated managers and employees about the parking situation at the head office. The parking lot quickly fills up, and annoyed employees spend large amounts of time searching for parking spaces in the neighbourhood. Many end up spending money on expensive parking meters or fines for illegal parking. As a consultant, you are asked to recommend a solution.

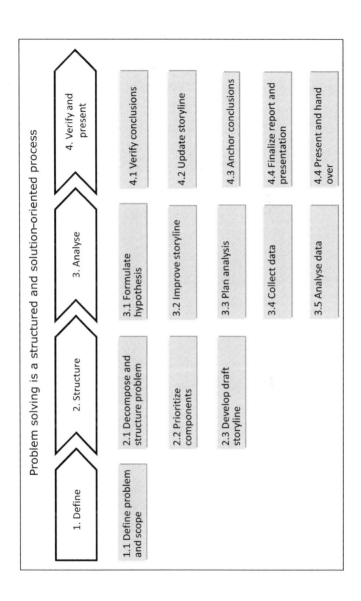

Problem solving is a structured and solution-oriented process

1. Define	2. Structure	3. Analyse	4. Verify and present
1.1 Define problem and scope	2.1 Decompose and structure problem	3.1 Formulate hypothesis	4.1 Verify conclusions
	2.2 Prioritize components	3.2 Improve storyline	4.2 Update storyline
	2.3 Develop draft storyline	3.3 Plan analysis	4.3 Anchor conclusions
		3.4 Collect data	4.4 Finalize report and presentation
		3.5 Analyse data	4.4 Present and hand over

3.3 Step 1. Defining the Problem

Before jumping in and finding possible solutions, it is important to make sure that you understand the problem. "A problem well stated is a problem half solved" (Charles Kettering, 1876–1958). Here are some checkpoints that can be used to study the problem and help define it:

- **Impact:** Before finding out *how* to solve a problem, you must understand *why* it is a problem. In this case, Linda explains that the frustration with the full parking lot has resulted in less satisfied employees and lower productivity.
- **Root cause:** You want to solve the problem and not just cover up the symptoms. The symptom in this case is lower employee satisfaction and frustration. A few interviews with managers and employees point back to the full parking lot.
- **Result:** How will you know when the problem is solved? In this case, it should be possible to measure the parking lot capacity and employee satisfaction or frustration level.

When you feel you have a good understanding of the problem, try to formulate it as a specific question. In this example, the problem could be formulated as, "How can we increase employee satisfaction by improving the parking situation?"

"And they want to know if I'm satisfied!"

3.4 Step 2. Structuring the Problem

Structure and Prioritize

When you have formulated the problem, addressing the root cause and impact, it has to be structured in such a way that possible solutions can be identified. A good tool is the "how-to" tree. This is a logical way of structuring suggested solutions in a top-down manner.

Be Lazy

Do as little as possible but as much as necessary. When solving problems, you want to work effectively (find the best solutions) and efficiently (not spending more resources than necessary).

MECE: The set of solutions should be mutually exclusive and collectively exhaustive. All possible solution sets have been identified—they are collectively exhaustive. The solutions should not overlap—they mutually exclude each other. In the final recommendations, you can combine solutions. In the example, to avoid a full parking lot, we can either increase the capacity or reduce the number of cars entering the lot. Or both.

Hypothesis-driven analysis: The solutions in the "How to" tree are hypotheses. This means we have to collect data and analyse the results before recommending a solution. A top-down structure will allow you to prioritize the work in the next step: analysis.

Solutions should be MECE with no gaps or overlaps

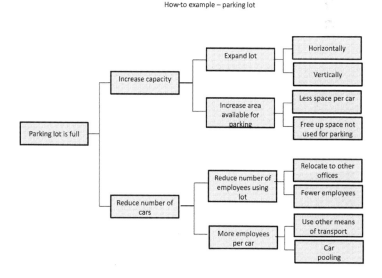

Solution 5

Solution 1

Solu-
tion 6

Solution 4

Solution 2

Solution 3

MECE: Mutually Exclusive, Collectively Exhaustive.

How-to example – parking lot

Parking lot is full

Increase capacity

Expand lot
- Horizontally
- Vertically

Increase area available for parking
- Less space per car
- Free up space not used for parking

Reduce number of cars

Reduce number of employees using lot
- Relocate to other offices
- Fewer employees

More employees per car
- Use other means of transport
- Car pooling

Develop the Storyline

The "how-to" solution hypothesis tree can be used to structure the storyline for the final report or presentation. It is a structured and logical way to present the problem with solution alternatives and support them with facts and analysis. The storyline can and should be used to communicate with stakeholders during the course of the project.

When asked about how work is progressing on the parking lot problem, you can easily communicate possible solutions and how you are working to confirm or discard them. "Linda, we're working with two sets of solutions. One set involves increasing the capacity in the lot. But we're also looking into ways of reducing the number of vehicles that are using the lot. The final recommendation may be a combination of the two."

In this way, you can get buy-in to recommendations early in the process and, at the same time, give others the possibility to come up with additional solutions that you may have missed. It's also easy to remember the story, which in turn makes it possible to have an ongoing dialogue about the problem and possible solutions. Everyone can join in.

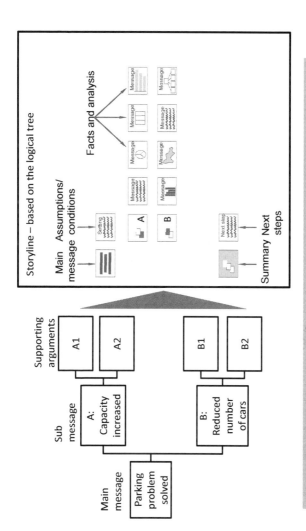

A well-structured logical tree underlines main messages and sells the recommendations

3.5 Step 3. Analysis

Planning Is Key

To secure that the analysis gets off to a good start, develop a good analysis plan that builds on the hypothesis solutions and storyline from step 2. The plan will visualize what analyses will be performed and how. You should also develop a timeline depicting who is responsible for each analysis, with clear deadlines. This will provide important insight into how much time is needed and which resources are required in the analysis work.

Hard and Soft Data Must Be Gathered

For each hypothesis, there will be a set of issues that have to be analysed. You now have to figure out which data are needed to verify or discard the suggested solution. Some of the data may be facts, like the number of employees driving to work and statistics for vehicles entering and exiting the lot.

These hard data may be available from a system, for example, a system registering activity into and out of the parking lot.

Other data may be softer, for example, how employees say they will react to the different solution alternatives. These soft data can be collected through interviews or questionnaires.

Analysis plan (example)

Problem/issue	Sub issue	Analysis required	Responsible/ sources	Due date
Increase capacity	Expand lot	Options for expanding lot horizontally or vertically	Facilities Dept.	31 August
	Increase area available for parking	Size of parking spaces. Possible to decrease size of each parking space and/or free up space not used for parking?	Facilities Dept.	15 September
Reduce number of cars	Reduce number of employees using lot	Number of employees driving in total and per car. Options for relocating staff to other offices with cost/benefit considerations. Head count reduction programs planned?	Human Resources Dept. / Finance Team	15 September
	More employees per car	Options for car pooling and/or use of other transport options	Compensatio n and Benefits Dept.	31 August

3.6 Step 4. Verification and Presentation

Verifying or Changing Solutions

As the analysis results come in, some of the original hypotheses will be verified as correct, while others must be discarded. It's important to have an open mind and not hold on to beliefs at all cost.

Finalizing Recommendations

Based on all the analysis, a final set of recommendations is developed. The storyline must be updated to reflect them, and the final report or presentation is developed.

Presenting the Final Result

The moment of truth (the proof of the pudding) comes when you stand before the customer, very often in a management, board, or steering committee meeting, and present the recommendations.

When preparing for the presentation, make sure to spend enough time on the presentation material: what you put in the slides, and what you use as speaking notes. You don't want to end up reading aloud what everyone can see on the screen.

Take time to rehearse in front of your team or a colleague. Get feedback on content, form, and your presentations skills. This will significantly improve the final presentation.

"And next year we'll do even better.
We'll need a bigger chart!"

3.7 The People Side of Problem Solving

It's Always a People Problem

No matter how it looks at first, it's always a people problem. What does it mean? Aren't the problem-solving tools and a structured process enough? The answer to the last question is, "Yes and No" To solve the right business problem, a structured approach and the right tools are invaluable.

But they are usually not enough.

Case: A back office department handling loan applications in a bank was getting complaints from account officers because of long lead times for processing the applications. The head of the department hired a consultant to look into the problem, which he thought was due to understaffing.

After a structured walkthrough, the consultant discovered that the root cause of the problem was varying quality on incoming applications. This variation caused unnecessary handovers back and forth between front and back office to ensure data quality. The solution was to get the front office staff to go the extra mile and make sure that all applications were filled in correctly before passing the application on to the back office. After proudly presenting these findings to the customer in a management meeting, the consultant received no thanks, and the contract was terminated.

"Maybe if we turn the chart around,
things will look better?"

Understanding How People Feel

Why did the consultant fail? The problem was analysed, the root cause identified, and a viable solution recommended. The reason is quite obvious: the consultant had not paid enough attention to the people side of the problem.

When presenting the solution in the management meeting, he had not addressed the problem of understaffing. Instead, he had identified a different problem. The department head felt incompetent (he did not understand a basic problem in his own department) and humiliated (his incompetence had been put on the table for all to see in the management meeting).

There are at least three lessons to be learned from this small example:

1. Involve the customer in the problem-definition phase to make sure that it is properly defined. This will give you buy-in to look at different causes and possible solutions.
2. Keep the customer in the loop during the problem-solving process. This will give the customer valuable insights.
3. Ask the customer if he prefers to present the results to the rest of management himself. This will ensure trust and open the door for future engagements. The customer understands that you are there to help him, not promote yourself.

CHAPTER 4

How to Manage Projects

4.1 Introduction to Project Management

Consultant engagements can vary and require a variety of approaches. But one thing is common: almost all consulting work is performed in a project setting.

A *project* is a temporary endeavour undertaken to meet a goal or objective, very often implying change. There is a defined beginning and end, and there are usually time and funding constraints and clearly defined deliverables.

Project management is the discipline of planning, organizing, securing, managing, leading, and controlling resources to achieve project goals within the defined constraints. Project management requires distinct skills and tools.

This chapter gives an overview of the five phases of a typical project and highlights the most important aspects of each project phase. It also provides a basic introduction to typical roles and responsibilities in a project.

As a consultant, you are expected to be an expert in project management. It is therefore necessary to invest in developing strong project management skills. The investment will pay dividends no matter what type of consulting you do.

The five-phase project model

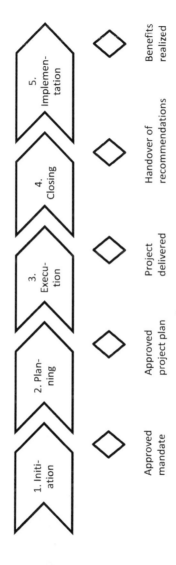

Phase	Milestone
1. Initiation	Approved mandate
2. Planning	Approved project plan
3. Execution	Project delivered
4. Closing	Handover of recommendations
5. Implementation	Benefits realized

4.2 Roles and Responsibilities

Although projects vary in size and complexity, the basic roles and responsibilities are the same.

Project Owner

- ensures ownership of and support for the project
- appoints a project manager

Steering Committee (Headed by the Project Owner)

- approves project mandate with objectives and plan
- allocates necessary resources
- makes decisions regarding scope, time, and resources when original boundaries are tested

Project Manager

- has overall responsibility for delivering the project results within agreed-upon constraints (time and resources)
- manages progress, quality, and resource usage
- reports to project owner or steering committee
- manages the project team

Project Participants

- perform assigned tasks
- cooperate with other project team members
- report problems or deviations to project manager

Typical project organization

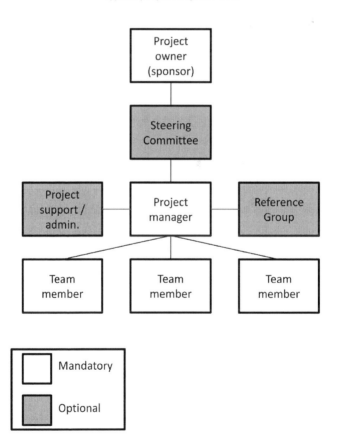

Some projects have additional roles:

Project Support and Administration

- complete project administrative tasks (developing templates, writing minutes, etc.) on behalf of the project manager

Reference Group

- function as important stakeholders who are not part of the steering committee or project group
- provide valuable input and insights to the project
- can serve as a sounding board for project recommendations
- when gathered as a group, discuss issues that impact several organizational units

4.3 Phase 1. Project Initiation

Good Mandate, Great Start

As a consultant, you will often be presented with a project mandate or asked to develop one on behalf of the project owner.

All endeavours deserve a good start. For projects, this is the initiation phase, resulting in an approved project mandate. Goals and objectives have to be clearly stated. It is critical that enough time is spent defining the business issue to be solved (see chapter 3). The conditions under which the project will operate have to be good enough. Constraints regarding scope, time, and resources must be identified.

Case: In 1911, in the famous race to the South Pole between the Norwegian Roald Amundsen and the Englishman Robert Scott, both teams set out at approximately the same time with the same goal. Amundsen reached the South Pole a month before Scott and returned without human casualties. No one from Scott's team returned alive. Although both teams spent plenty of time preparing, they chose very different strategies. For transportation, Amundsen chose dogs while Scott chose motor sledges and ponies. Many of the problems of Scott's team can be traced back to the decisions made in the initiation phase of the journey, but the problems increased during the next phases of the race.

Be Patient, Get the Mandate Right

A good project mandate must be clear on the following:

1. What business problem is the project going to solve (the project goal), and for whom (the project owner)?
2. What are the deliverables (in other words, the results of the project)?
3. What are the major milestones? These are the points on the project timeline when key decisions are made or important deliverables developed.
4. Is there a sufficiently good business case? Who is responsible for realizing the benefits (increased sales, lower costs, etc.) in the business case?
5. Do we have the necessary resources (budget and people, skills and capacity)?
6. Does the project have the necessary priority and management attention? Are we competing with other projects for resources and attention?
7. How will the project be organized? Who will be the project manager? Who will be on the project team? How will other important stakeholders be involved?

Sometimes, there will be pressure to start project work quickly. This should raise warning flags. If the mandate is unclear, do not proceed into the next phase of the project. Perhaps you need a scoping subphase, typically spending two to three weeks with the key stakeholders working out the mandate. This is definitely time well spent. If the mandate questions are not answered up front, they will drain energy and focus later.

"We have a rough outline of what we want to achieve. Let's get the project up and running and get to work. We'll finish the mandate as we go forward."

From Project to Program Management

The issue or problem at hand may be so complex or large that several projects have to be established to solve it holistically. This is called a program, and a program-management approach is required.

For example, a new Customer Relationship Management (CRM) solution will typically require a business process design project and an IT development project, each with clear project mandates. The two projects will often be coordinated by a program management team to ensure a holistic approach.

To become a good program manager, it's a big advantage to have extensive project management experience, preferably from different types of projects. Change management capabilities are an integral part of the program manager's skill set.

Critical Success Factors for Project Initiation

In conclusion, the critical success factors for the initiation phase are

- a clearly defined project mandate,
- an engaged project owner,
- a sound business case and high priority, and
- the necessary resources and right organization.

4.4 Phase 2. Project Planning

Planning Is Vital

A good project initiation has to be followed up by solid planning.

In the planning phase, you may even discover that the mandate has to be changed.

Case: In the race for the South Pole, Robert Scott decided to use motor sledges and ponies in addition to manual hauling of sledges (Amundsen chose dogs). Unfortunately, and at least partly due to insufficient planning, Scott didn't bring along the engineer who had created and tested the motor sledges. So when the sledges failed during the expedition, there was no one on the team with sufficient knowledge to repair them.

Scott made some other planning mistakes:

- *Cross-country ski training was recommended for all but not compulsory.*
- *There was an insufficient number of depots for food, drink, and fuel, and the depots were not marked well enough.*
- *Food supplies lacked the necessary vitamins.*
- *Fuel cans were not properly protected, causing leakages.*

"There's never a good mechanic
around when you need one."

Establishing the Project Group

After the project mandate has been approved by the project owner, the project group must be established. These are the core resources that have the necessary skills and capacity to drive the project forward.

The participants must be briefed by their managers on their role in the project and how much time they will use. As a general rule, project participants should have at least 50 per cent of their time prioritized for project work. This is necessary to ensure sufficient capacity to do actual work. With less than 50 per cent availability, there will only be time to participate in meetings and give input to materials produced by others.

The project group must not be too big. Five to seven people is often a good number, manageable in size whilst having good production capacity. If more people have to be involved, it is wise to consider establishing subgroups (focusing on specific topics) or setting up a reference group.

As a consultant, you are expected to be an experienced project participant. You will very often be the project manager, responsible for driving the project forward on behalf of the project owner.

"Pick me for the team! I write great minutes!"

Project Kick-Off

At the beginning of the project, it is important to get participants onboard, both collectively and individually. To ensure a good start for the team, hold a kick-off meeting.

The main objective with the kick-off meeting is to make sure that the project group understands the goals and objectives of the project and how the group will work to achieve them. Everyone has to understand their role and how they will contribute to the success of the project. Do a walkthrough of the project mandate. The team will often have valuable input regarding details in the mandate, requiring an update after the kick-off meeting.

The kick-off meeting is a great way for project group members to get to know each other and begin working together. I recommend holding the kick-off meeting offsite, for example at a hotel, with an agenda going from lunch day 1 to lunch day 2. This will create a more relaxed environment, accommodate team work (start working on the project plan), and encourage socializing.

As a consultant, you will often be in charge of the project kick-off on behalf of the project owner. You will probably be responsible for preparing the agenda, sending out the invitations, and seeing that the logistics (meeting facilities, documents, etc.) are handled smoothly.

"Welcome to the kick-off, everyone. I'm really looking forward to working with you here at beautiful Milestone Lodge!"

Project Support and Administration

Project administrative tasks will more often than not be handled by the consultant. This includes

- developing the detailed project plan;
- developing the necessary documentation templates;
- meeting administration including invitations, preparatory documentation, leading or facilitating meetings and workshops, and preparing minutes;
- monitoring and reporting progress; and
- assembling the delivery documents of the project.

Detailed Planning

In the planning phase, the project group develops a detailed delivery plan (breakdown of the project milestones). Responsibility for deliverables and tasks is distributed to the team members based on their individual skills, capacity, and role in the organization.

During detailed planning, you will often discover that more resources are required in the project group. This is a natural consequence of a more detailed understanding of the depth and breadth of the work that you get when breaking down milestones into concrete activities and tasks. These resource issues must be resolved as quickly as possible with the project owner or steering group.

"After completing these minutes, I'd better call
Linda and set up a new project meeting."

Reporting and Follow-Up

A clear reporting structure must be developed. The project team will normally meet once a week at a minimum, following up progress on the project plan, discussing work in progress, and resolving issues on a continuous basis. Minutes should be made after each meeting, documenting decisions made and actions to be followed up by the team members.

Involve the project owner on a regular basis. In addition to formal and informal meetings, it is common to have a steering group with the project owner and key stakeholders. The project owner will usually lead the steering group. A steering group typically meets monthly and is given a status report on progress, resource usage, risks, and any major issues that must be clarified. Their job is to help the project manager, so it is important to establish an honest dialogue with them.

Communication and Involvement

A project living on its own in a bubble is not good. It must be on the management agenda throughout the project life cycle. A good communication plan (developed in the planning phase) will specify who needs to be involved when and how.

If involvement and communication are critical for project success, one of the project members should come from the internal communications department.

Communication plan (example)

Stakeholder	What	How	Who	When
Top management	Commitment to support Progress and key issues	Top management meetings and status reports	Project owner	Monthly
Management teams of affected departments	Rationale for project How affected and involved Progress and key issues	Management meetings Brain storming workshop	Project owner / project manager	Initiation phase Monthly
Employees in affected departments	Rationale for project How affected and involved Progress and key issues	Intranet articles Departmental meetings Frequently Asked Questions Intranet	Project owner / project manager	Initiation phase Continually
Union	Staffing consequences Key issues	Meeting	Project owner + CEO?	Initiation phase
Human resources	Staffing consequences Change and training requirements	Meeting with HR management HR part of project team?	Project owner / project manager	Initiation phase
IT	IT requirements	Meeting with IT management IT part of project team?	Project owner / project manager	Initiation phase

Engagement of Stakeholders

It will almost always be necessary to engage people outside the project group to collect data, provide input on solution ideas, and plan implementation efforts. These stakeholders or reference persons must be interviewed, invited to workshops, or give their input through surveys.

On occasion, it may be a good idea to gather the reference persons in a group setting (reference group). This should be done when consensus around deliverables across different organizational units is required; it is important to have open discussions and not just collect individual inputs.

The Devil Is in the Details

Make sure that activities are broken down to a detailed level. This is important to ensure agreement on what is to be done, by whom, and when. Only then is it possible to check that the project has sufficient resources and a realistic timeline. This again will ease progress management.

Detailed planning is nitty-gritty work that requires experience and skill. People are on average too optimistic. We think that tasks are easier than they are and that they will be performed quicker than is really possible. It is therefore a good idea to build reserves into the plan, both in the budget (10 to 20 per cent for most projects) and the timeline.

"What do they mean? I'm not in anyone's details!"

Risk Management

Risk management is an area where most project managers can improve their skills. In the planning phase, the major risks of the project must be identified. Typical risks are

- insufficient resources (quantity or quality),
- delays in deliveries from units outside the project's chain of command (for example, software vendors), and
- changes in requirements or constraints (for example, additional regulatory reporting).

A risk analysis and mitigation plan should be signed off by the project owner as early as possible. For each risk, the probability must be estimated and the consequences understood. Each risk must be mitigated by actions that will reduce either probability or consequences. The mitigation actions should be integrated in the project plan.

The risk analysis must be followed up frequently in the project group. It is also an excellent way of communicating with the project owner or steering committee, providing them with a tool for making important decisions for the project.

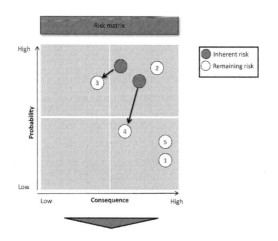

Risk mitigation plan (example)

#	Risk description	Risk mitigation	Respon-sible	Deadline	Status
1	Delay in software from external vendor	• Tight follow up of vendor	IT	• Continually	• Open
2	Complex solution - delays and cost over runs	• External quality assurance reviews • Tight follow up of progress and quality	Project manager	• Monthly • Weekly	• Open • Open
3	Lack of union support	• Involve union repr. In steering committee	Project owner	• Initiation phase	• Closed
4	Resource conflicts with other projects	• Resource agreements • Tight follow up of resource availability	Project manager	• Initiation phase • Continually	• Closed • In progress
5	Competitive environment changes drastically and makes project obsolete	• Track competitors and market	Corporate strategy team	• Quarterly	•In progress

Critical Success Factors

In conclusion, the critical success factors for the planning phase are

- a detailed work plan and risk analysis,
- well-defined roles and responsibilities, and
- realistic time estimates and a sound timeline.

4.5 Phase 3. Project Execution

From Planning to Doing

It is now time to perform the tasks defined in the project plan. The individual members of the project group will start working on their tasks. These will, of course, vary depending on what type of project you're executing. A business strategy project will have a completely different set of tasks than a systems development project.

As a consultant, you may have a purely advisory role or clearly defined tasks. Often, you will be in charge of a project or subproject. Developing project management skills is therefore a fundamental part of the consulting toolkit. Formal training in tools and techniques is recommended in combination with extensive on-the-job training.

The Importance of the Team

As project manager, you are 100 per cent dependent on your team. Team selection is usually done in the planning phase, but often additional team members will join the team in the execution phase. If possible, make sure that the team members have the necessary technical (business and functional) skills to perform their designated tasks. Your job as project manager is to get the best out of your team.

But equally as important are their interpersonal skills. Why? Because the team must have a constructive and collaborative way of working to succeed. Individuals have to be able to work together in the project group. They are also ambassadors for the project to the rest of the organization. This means that they as a rule must speak positively about the project and interact with people outside the project group to collect input, perform information activities, and so on.

Handling Team Issues

Because the team is essential to project success, the temperature of the team should be measured on a regular basis. If you sense that things are not as they should be, take action quickly. Symptoms of this problem include

- deviations from plan (progress, quality, or costs),
- an aggressive tone between members in meetings, and
- sickness or absence.

If you discover that the problem is isolated to one individual, he or she should be replaced. If there is a relationship problem between two or more individuals, you may be able to resolve this by clarifying the cause of the problem and helping them find a solution that they can accept. Under no circumstance must the team spirit be allowed to deteriorate over time. Find the cancer, cure it, or remove it!

"Stop quarreling, guys. We're going
to miss the deadline."

Monitoring and Follow-Up

I am not a big fan of Vladimir Lenin, the Soviet dictator. But one Lenin quote that you should remember is this: "Trust is good, control is better." To secure timely and high-quality deliverables, a certain amount of control is needed. One control mechanism for a project group is the weekly status meeting—preferably with written minutes.

The following must be covered in status meetings:

- A follow-up of action points from the previous meeting
- Status of subprojects or areas of responsibility:
    o deliveries the previous week (celebrate often!)
    o plans for the week to come
    o deviations (progress, quality, cost) from plan
    o issues that need to be discussed in the group

In project meetings and monthly steering group meetings, potential problems or deviations must be visualized and addressed. This is like going to the dentist. The toothache seldom disappears by itself, and the longer you postpone your dentist appointment, the more painful it will be. If you wait too long, the tooth may have to be pulled out.

Knowing When to Stop

Even though your project shows a positive business case and gets high priority, circumstances change. New customer demands, additional resource constraints, or changes in strategy may change the business case for the project. We seldom stop projects. There is a tendency (maybe it's human nature?) to finish what we have started.

Case: In the race for the South Pole, Robert Scott pushed forward even though he saw the risks regarding rations and fuel for the return journey. If he had stopped in time and given up the quest for the pole, he and his team most probably would have survived. Instead, he continued, with severe weather and illness among team members slowing the team down. More often than with Amundsen's team, there were days when there was no travelling at all. Lack of fuel also meant that snow could not be melted in large enough quantities, causing dehydration. The last team members died only eleven miles from the final depot.

We must regularly check that the foundation for continuing the project is solid. As a consultant, you must speak out if you believe termination should be considered. Resources are scarce and deserve to be used where they give the best return on investment for the organization.

Critical Success Factors

In conclusion, the critical success factors for the execution phase are

- a collaborative and dedicated team,
- continuous involvement and information,
- frequent follow-up,
- risk management,
- early escalation of potential problems, and
- terminate the project in time if necessary.

4.6 Phase 4. Project Closing

Going the Last Mile

When all deliverables have been completed (hopefully on time, within budget, and with the predefined qualities), the project must be closed down professionally. This phase is often handled poorly. Project participants are eager to get on with the next project or return to their regular jobs.

Close the project properly. For large and complex projects, write an evaluation report. Gather all project participants and steering group members to a summary workshop and answer questions such as these:

- Did the project reach the overall objectives?
- What did the project do right and what contributed to the success of the project?
- Were there any tasks that could have been performed better?
- How did the team work, and should others have been involved more closely?
- Has new knowledge or a best practice been developed, and how can the organization leverage this?

All these lessons learned are important for the individual, the group, and the organization to discuss and understand.

Celebrate the Success of the Project

Finally, don't forget to celebrate. Take the team out to dinner or reward them in some other way. Make sure to thank everyone for their hard work and contributions to the success of the project.

"For a while we were stinking together.
I prefer drinking together!"

Critical Success Factors

In conclusion, the critical success factors for the closing phase are

- verifying that the objectives were reached,
- capturing lessons learned and possible best practices,
- acknowledging individual and group contributions, and
- celebrating!

4.7 Phase 5. Implementation

It Ain't over 'til the Fat Lady Sings

The project is not really over until recommendations have been implemented and the benefits from the business case realized. However, in many organizations, line management is responsible for implementing the recommendations made by the project as part of business as usual.

In my view, implementation and benefits realization should be done as a separate project phase, and participants from the execution phase should be closely involved. Otherwise continuity will be lacking, and there is a considerable probability that implementation will suffer. Benefits will evaporate, and the project can quickly fail (or at least not be as successful as it could have been).

Implementation: Learning by Doing

Implementing and realizing benefits is the whole point of the project and of consultation. Yet this is where so many fail. There is a clear difference in knowing what to do and knowing how to do it. Much of the criticism towards consultants is related to failure during implementation. Translating recommendations into practical actions requires skill and experience. It is therefore essential that consultants have implementation experience.

The consultant will usually have a limited role during implementation. The owner of the business case will be responsible for the implementation and will either act as project manager in this phase or use a direct report. As a consultant, you may have the role of sparring partner or have responsibility for certain tasks, for example, training or administrative support in following up the action plan.

Involve the People Affected by the Results

As consultants, we often over-rationalize the "whats" and view them as isolated from the project's perspective. A holistic, people-oriented approach is required to succeed with change (implementation usually implies changing the way people work).

By holistic, I mean that the recommended solution (the "whats") must be viewed from the perspective of the organization and individual employee. As discussed earlier, the best way to achieve this is to involve the affected department managers and employees from beginning to end, especially in implementation planning. This way, you will get the "hows" right.

Reaping the Benefits

Implementation is an endurance sport. Persistence is essential when implementing recommendations, especially when it comes to benefits. To reap the benefits of a new sales system, training all users in the system is fundamental. But changing the work culture by setting new sales targets, measuring effects, and rewarding the sales champion will secure lasting benefits. The manager who owns the business case is responsible for implementing the project recommendations and realizing the business benefits.

After a period of time, realized benefits must be measured against the original business case. Did the new solution deliver the promised results to the business? The owner of the business case must sign off and report back to the management level that initiated the project. Then the project life cycle will be complete.

Critical Success Factors

In conclusion, the critical success factors for the implementation phase are

- participants from the execution phase must follow the project all the way through to implementation,

- affected managers and employees must be involved in implementation planning,
- implementation must be rigorous and holistic, and
- benefits must be evaluated against the business case, and management must sign off to indicate that benefits have been realized.

"I'm off to deliver the low-hanging fruits! Keep picking the high-hanging ones!"

CHAPTER 5

How to Develop and Grow as a Consultant

5.1 Prepare a Development Plan

Why Do You Need a Plan?

One of the great things about consulting is the possibility for continuous learning. New customers, new industries, new problems to solve, and new team constellations create ever-changing learning arenas.

To ensure that your development has a direction, take responsibility for your own learning and growth. Prepare your own development plan. In addition to giving your development direction, a development plan is a tool that enables you to keep yourself up to date and more attractive by continually learning new skills and broadening your knowledge base.

Development Planning in Three Steps

To make a good plan for your own development, try to think of yourself as a business. Why? Because business and consulting are continually changing. It's also more fun!

Step 1. Assessment

What are your main strengths as a consultant? These are the core features that your success will be built upon. What are the key weaknesses (if any) that you should address?

Step 2. Goals

What are your development goals, both short term (the next six to twelve months) and long term (two to five years)?

Step 3. Action plan

Which steps must be taken to reach your goals? What kind of project should you try to get on, and which skills will you try to develop on each of them? Which training courses should you take to get new knowledge?

When developing your plan, make sure to have goals. Goals should be SMART (Specific, Measurable, Attractive, Relevant, Time-bound).

Development plan (template)

		Strengths		Weaknesses	
Step 1 - Assessment					
	Area	Short term (6-12 months)		Long term (2-5 years)	
Step 2 - Goals	Role/ position				
	Expertise				
	Personal skills / leadership				
	Area	Actions (Projects & training)	Timeframe	Status	
Step 3 – Action plan	Role/ position				
	Expertise				
	Personal skills / leadership				

5.2 Expertise: Breadth and Depth

Be Saleable!

Being a management consultant is not just a career, it's also a business. You have to be saleable to different clients in several industries and functions. To do this, you need more than one area of expertise.

This is also a risk-reduction measure. When there is no longer a need for your services at one client, you'll have other options.

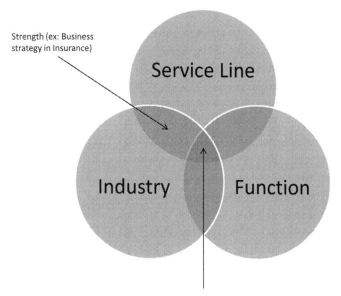

Strength (ex: Business strategy in Insurance)

Service Line

Industry   Function

Uniqueness (ex: Process Improvement in Finance Function in Banking)

Service Line

Your core competencies as a consultant will be within one or more consulting service lines. The main reason that clients will hire you as a consultant is your ability to help solve their unique business problems with skills that are not available within their organization.

No matter which service line you focus on (strategy development, change management, project management, etc.), make sure to be really good at it.

Industry Knowledge

I usually recommend consultants focus on deep knowledge of an industry, for example, financial services or telecommunications. Within that industry, work for several customers on different engagements and in several functional areas.

Deep knowledge does not mean that you have to be an expert in all aspects of the client's industry. But you should have good understanding of how the industry works, the basic business model(s), key trends, and important issues.

Why? Because you need this knowledge to be able to communicate with the client and be a good consultant.

Functional Knowledge

It is wise to also have expertise in a functional area that crosses industry boundaries, for example, finance or IT.

Why? It enables you to work in several industries, gaining valuable insights that provide value for your customers through knowledge transfer.

5.3 Continuous Training and Development

A consulting career is an opportunity for lifelong learning. No two situations are the same. The business challenges for your clients may be similar, but each client—its organization, culture, people—will be unique.

On-the-Job Learning: The Project Is the Key!

Each engagement or project is a chance to learn new skills; either business skills, technical skills, or interpersonal skills. Based on your development plan, define the specific learning areas for every project you work on. Throughout your consulting career, most of the learning will happen on the job, through the projects you work on.

Courses and Training

Spice up your continuous on-the-job training by attending seminars and courses. This will keep your service line knowledge up to date by exposing yourself to the latest frameworks, methods, and techniques. You should also try to attend industry seminars and functional courses to be on top of best practices and industry trends. This will also allow you to discuss issues with colleagues and meet potential clients.

Ideally, the courses should be chosen according to the project portfolio you are working on or forthcoming projects in your pipeline. Then you will get synergies by combining theory with practical hands-on training.

Start with the Basics

In the beginning of your consulting career, your focus will be on building basic consulting skills. Over time, you should build your areas of expertise based on what kind of work you enjoy and succeed at. You can expand these areas in the future.

Get Implementation Experience

To be able to give credible advice, clients expect you to have hands-on experience. How else can they trust your recommendations? You can't just say, "I think this will work." Your advice becomes trustworthy when you can draw on your own real-life experiences. They don't have to be from an identical situation (this is seldom possible, because all clients are unique). But it does help if you can document that you actually have implemented a strategy, an IT solution, a process redesign, or an outsourcing agreement.

My advice, therefore, is get lots of implementation experience from different areas. You never know when it will come in handy, but it will be useful at some point.

Use Feedback to Improve

Ask for periodic assessment and feedback on your work. Your ability to accept and integrate honest feedback will ensure that you become a better consultant and that you get repeat engagements.

CHAPTER 6

A New Consulting Reality?

6.1 Consulting: An Evolving Industry

During the last few decades, major developments have affected the consulting industry. In sum, they push consulting innovation. The competitive advantage of yesterday has become a necessity of today.

Diversification

As the large global consulting firms have pursued continuous growth, new service concepts have evolved. One of the most important is business process outsourcing (BPO).

Accenture and others have used their industry, functional, and delivery capabilities to take over finance, IT, and other support functions from large corporations. The service provider achieves economies of scale and can deliver quality services, at a lower price, back to the business.

The corporation frees up management time and resources to focus on core business activities. Support functions can be moved around the world by the service provider, depending on where the optimal quality and cost can be achieved. These effects can also be taken out by global corporations without the use of service providers, achieving full control but tying up significant management resources.

Internal Consulting Units

Back in the 1970s, some large corporations had already established internal consulting units. Today, it's quite common to have these types of units. Some Fortune 500 companies that have such units are American Express, General Electric, Sara Lee, Pepsico, and JPMorgan Chase. Two examples in the European banking industry are Den Norske Bank (DNB) in Norway and UniCredit in Italy.

There are several reasons for the internal consultancy trend:

- **The power of the consulting approach.** Instead of relying solely on external providers, establishing an internal consulting unit makes these services more accessible within the organization.
- **The internal perspective.** This is the intimate knowledge of the organization's people, practices, and management style. This saves time when figuring out the whos and hows of problem solving and implementation.
- **Costs.** Significantly lower consulting costs are another nice benefit from internal consulting.
- **Knowledge management.** Knowledge is developed and skills are kept in house, not in the heads of external consultants, who then

can sell this expertise to other companies (even competitors).

- **Recruiting and talent management.** Some companies, like DNB, view internal consulting units as important tools in recruiting and developing talent. These units are attractive entry points for external consultants and university graduates looking for a career in a large corporation. They quickly get a good top-down overview of the business in combination with insights into the different business and support units. Equipped with this organizational knowledge and a solution-oriented consulting approach, they can move into management positions, often headhunted by the units that have used them on strategic projects. These organizations see the value of managers possessing consulting skills.

"The new line of consultants is ready to be launched."

6.2 Consulting 2.0

Consulting 1.0: A Dying Business Model?

Consulting has evolved over the decades, but the business model has for the most part stayed the same, at least among the largest consulting firms:

- The pyramid-based consulting team (partner, manager, senior, consultant, and analyst) is still the most common delivery model.
- The consulting team collects input from inside and outside the organization, performs analyses, and delivers a recommendation to the customer.

This model will still be used from time to time, when a company lacks the necessary capabilities or it is vital that a completely fresh outside view is required to solve the business problem. But the model is not sustainable for the whole consulting industry.

New Business Models Are in the Making

With the Internet and refined search engines like Google, information is at everyone's fingertips. Historically, this was one of the important benefits of using external consultants: learning from their experiences as professionals and consultants for other clients. This is still the case to some degree. However, a continuous stream of industry and functional conferences, as well as the Internet, make it possible to tap more easily into knowledge and experiences from around the globe.

Many companies have strong strategic and analysis capabilities, and many managers have consulting and project management experience. These companies will not be willing to pay big bucks for consultants to learn their business. They will either expect concrete value-added services or the ability to cherry-pick which consultants they work with.

So how can consultants create value in this new consulting reality?

Specialization

One option is specialization. Some firms specialize in competitive intelligence and benchmarking. This is a value-added service, enabling companies to measure themselves against competitors in order to identify weaknesses and strengths, thereby enabling them to sharpen their strategies.

Collaborative Working Model

Another option is to develop a collaborative working model. This means setting up joint teams with members from the customer and consulting organization working side by side and bringing in skills that complement each other. The consultant may be the project manager, but he or she will be expected to lead the team towards a common goal, and the result will be a joint effort.

Explorative and Iterative Mentality

Speed and time to market are becoming increasingly important. The traditional consultancy project spanning several months will in many cases be replaced by a more explorative and iterative approach. Instead of analysing problems to death, finding "good enough" solutions and piloting them will be the new normal in many cases.

Pricing Revisited

Pricing schemes will be challenged. The traditional "time and material" and fixed fee contracts may be replaced by a value-added or risk/reward model where the consultants are not paid unless the results are in line with (or above) expectations.

The Future of Consulting Is Exciting

And what will happen in the years to come with the explosive development in technology and disbursement of devices? We will see the development of "on-demand consulting" with online interactive consulting services and consulting apps.

The traditional consulting business models will continue to be challenged in new and innovative ways. But there will always be a market for consultants who adapt to this ever-changing environment.

"The new consulting reality is challenging."

Conclusion

You have reached the end of the book. You are now equipped with a good understanding of how to succeed as a management consultant.

A career in management consulting will continually challenge you and provide you with opportunities to learn and grow. You will solve complex business problems and work in dynamic project structures to help businesses change to become more successful. Each day will differ from the one before.

As a consultant, you must take charge of your own development to ensure that your skills, knowledge, and work methods are up to date and state of the art.

The consulting way of working is powerful, whether you decide to pursue a career in management consulting or choose ordinary management positions in business or the public sector. The skills of problem solving and project management will serve you well. I urge you to learn and use them.

If you have become inspired to read more about management consulting, I refer you to my recommended reading list.

Acknowledgements

All successful projects are a team effort. Special thanks go to the main contributors:

My employer, Den Norske Bank, gave me a three-month leave of absence to get the project going.

My colleague Benedicta Aall Bugge patiently read early drafts of the text and provided valuable input.

Magnus Hermstad quickly understood the concept of the book and did a great job bringing it to life through his illustrations.

My wife, Trine, and the rest of the family had confidence in the endeavour, and they supported me from start to finish. Without their support, I never would have set out on this journey.

Erik Gausel, June 2013

Where Can I Read More?

If you want to read more consulting-oriented literature, here are a few books that I recommend.

Consulting Profession

Biswas, Sugata, and Daryl Twitchell, *Management Consulting: A Complete Guide to the Industry* (New York, 2002).

Block, Peter, *Flawless Consulting* (2nd edn, San Francisco, 2000).

Kubr, Milan, *Management Consulting: A Guide to the Profession* (4th edn, New Dehli, 2002).

Nelson, Bob, and Peter Economy, *Consulting for Dummies* (Indianapolis, 2008).

Rasiel, Ethan M., *The McKinsey Way* (New York, 1999).

Roos, Göran, and Steinar Bjørtveit, *Scandinavian Perspectives on Consulting* (Oslo, 2005).

Weinberg, Gerald M., *The Secrets of Consulting: A Guide to Giving and Receiving Advice Successfully* (New York, 1985).

Tools and Techniques

Andler, Nicolai, *Tools for Project Management, Workshops and Consulting* (Erlangen, 2008).

Doyle, Michael, and David Straus, *How to Make Meetings Work* (New York, 1976).

Graham, Nick, and Stanley E. Portny, *Project Management for Dummies* (West Sussex, 2011).

Printed in Great Britain
by Amazon